ANCIENT CIVILIZATIONS
The Vikings

by Tristan Boyer Binns

COMPASS POINT BOOKS MINNEAPOLIS, MINNESOTA

First American edition published in 2006 by
Compass Point Books
3109 West 50th St., #115
Minneapolis, MN 55410

THE VIKINGS
was produced by
David West Children's Books
7 Princeton Court
55 Felsham Road
London SW15 1AZ

Illustrator: Ross Watton
Designer: Gary Jeffrey
Editors: Kate Newport, Nick Healy
Page Production: Bobbie Nuytten
Content Adviser: Terje Leiren,
   Professor and Chair, Department of Scandinavian Studies,
   University of Washington

Visit Compass Point Books on the Internet at
www.compasspointbooks.com
or e-mail your request to
custserv@compasspointbooks.com

Library of Congress Cataloging-in-Publication Data
Binns, Tristan Boyer, 1968-
   The Vikings / by Tristan Boyer Binns.
      p. cm.—(Ancient civilization)
   Includes bibliographical references and index.
   ISBN 0-7565-1678-1 (hard cover)
   1. Vikings—Juvenile literature. 2. Norsemen—Juvenile literature. 3. Civilization, Viking—Juvenile literature. I. Title. II. Ancient civilizations (Minneapolis, Minn.)
   DL65.B525 2006
   948'.022—dc22   2005025058

   ISBN 0-7565-1760-5 (paperback)

Contents

The Vikings

The Vikings did not come from one country. They were all from Scandinavia, but their lands were different. Some areas had many mountains, while others had forests or land where crops would not grow. They had to find new ways to support their families, so they went raiding and settling foreign lands. Vikings all spoke one language, Old Norse. They shared the same culture and beliefs. Although the Vikings lived more than 1,000 years ago, we know a lot about their lives.

Look for this man digging up interesting items from the past, like this Viking helmet.

The Viking World

Vikings came from Norway, Sweden, and Denmark. They raided, traded, and settled in many lands—some of them thousands of miles away. Vikings were very loyal to their families. A chief led groups of families on raids and in battles. Any rewards were shared equally.

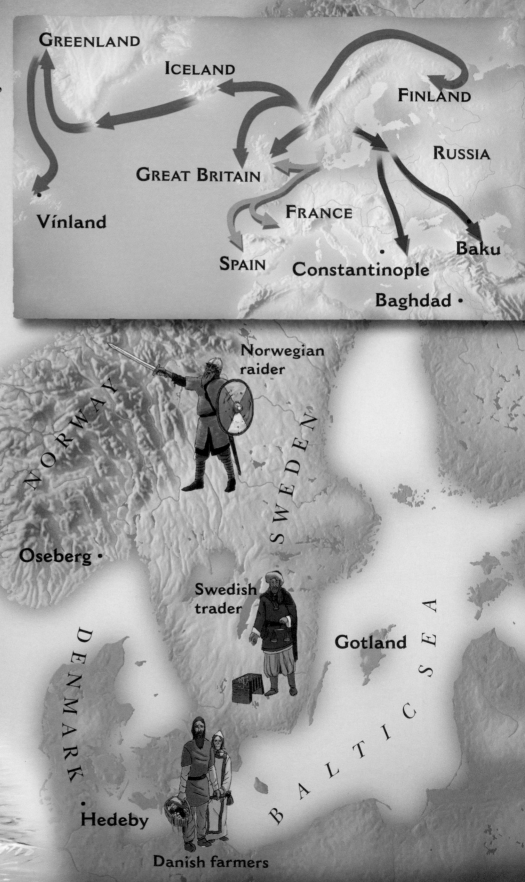

GREENLAND

ICELAND

FINLAND

RUSSIA

GREAT BRITAIN

Vínland

FRANCE

Baku

SPAIN

Constantinople

Baghdad

Norwegian raider

NORWAY

SWEDEN

Oseberg

Swedish trader

Gotland

NORTH SEA

DENMARK

BALTIC SEA

Hedeby

Danish farmers

Strong Vikings became kings. They ruled many chiefs, and sometimes more than one country. Viking rulers were called jarls. Free men and women were called karls. There were also slaves, called thralls. They could buy their freedom with hard work.

All Vikings had to go to twice-yearly meetings called Things. New laws were made and criminals were tried there. Fun was had as well, with wrestling matches and shopping in local markets.

Runes were Viking letters. Rune stones, like one in Sweden (left), were carved when somebody died. The writing around the outside is about their life.

If one Viking killed another, he had to pay a fine called wergeld to make it up to his victim's family.

Viking Families

For Vikings, families were the most important thing in their lives. They would fight to the death for each other. Homes could have parents, grandparents, and children, as well as some slaves.

Most men were farmers, fishermen, or craftsmen. They only went to raid for short periods of the year. Women ran the households. Children didn't go to school.

Vikings didn't have soap. They sweated dirt off their bodies in saunas. The ammonia in cow urine got clothes clean—but it was smelly!

Over the top of their long dresses, women wore apron-like overdresses. They were held on with decorative metal pins such as the one above.

Boys and girls learned to fight and helped with the chores. Boys 15 and sometimes younger could go on raids. At 15, girls could marry.

Viking houses had one long room with a fire in the middle. Women spent a lot of time around the fire, cooking, weaving, and looking after the children. Houses were dark and smoky because they had no windows or chimneys. People slept on benches built into the walls.

On the Farm

Vikings ate twice a day—in the morning and in the evening. They had to find or grow what they ate. They picked wild fruits and hunted wild animals and fish. They grew grains, vegetables, and fruits on their farms.

Most Viking farmers knew how to work with iron. Many lived far from towns, so they had to make and repair their farm tools by themselves.

Viking houses all looked the same, but sometimes what they were made from changed. People who lived in forests built their houses from wood. People who lived on the plains built sod houses with grass roofs.

Vikings kept animals such as pigs, cows, sheep, goats, ducks, and hens for food. The animals also gave wool, feathers, and skins to make clothes and pillows. In the spring, the crops were planted. In the autumn, they were harvested. Fresh food was dried or smoked to keep it good through the winter.

Bread was mostly made from barley, rye, or oats. When times were hard, it was made from bitter bark and acorns.

Viking Ships

Almost every Viking man knew how to sail a ship. Ships were their main form of transportation. Sailing was fast, easy, and safe. Viking ships were the best in Europe. They could move and turn more quickly than any others.

The famous Viking longship was built for war. It could carry raiders across open seas, then right up onto land.

Carved dragons and serpents were sometimes fixed to the fronts of the longships. They terrified Viking enemies as they sailed into view.

Viking ships were wide, to keep them stable. They were also shallow, so they could go far up rivers and right up onto beaches.

Longships had large sails, but they also had oars for when the winds dropped. Knarrs, or cargo ships, used sails for power. They could carry 25 tons of cargo across the ocean. Small work ships were used for short distances and for fishing.

Master shipbuilders used oak, pine, and birch trees. They carefully split the logs into planks and chiseled them into shape. A ship had a keel running its whole length. Planks made the sides. Ribs joined across the middle.

Viking Attack!

In 793, more than 1,200 years ago, Vikings raided the monastery at Lindisfarne in England. From then on, Vikings raided all over Europe. They went in small groups or in big parties to take treasure, food, animals, and slaves.

They won because they did not fear death. They were brutal and ruthless. Their swords, axes, bows, and spears were among the best weapons of the times. Young men often went raiding to get land and wealth, then set up homes and farms.

Most Viking raiders attacked by sea. They leapt straight from their ships and into battle. This surprised and terrified their victims. Vikings had wooden shields and armor made from leather or chain mail.

Vikings fought each other, too. Duels were fought on a small square of cloth. If you stepped off the cloth, you were a coward.

An early Viking helmet was made from metal plates joined together. **The piece at the front was to protect the nose.**

Exploring

Vikings were running out of good farmland at home. Brave explorers found new lands to settle. Some were easy to take over, such as Iceland and Greenland. Others had native people the Vikings had to defeat first.

Vikings first moved into England, Scotland, Ireland, and France as raiders. Over time, they made homes, brought their families over, and married local people.

Erik the Red brought settlers to Greenland 1,000 years ago. For 500 years, Vikings survived there. Finally the harsh winters and famine drove them away.

People sailed for weeks across rough seas in open boats. They had no compasses or maps, so they had to steer by the stars. They landed in their new homes wet, hungry, and often sick.

The Vikings kept many of their traditions, but they had to change what they farmed and hunted to suit the new land. They left behind carvings, burials, and even their language. English still uses Norse words today, such as *husband* and *window*.

Vikings brought their way of life to new lands. A comb and needle from York, England, were made the same way as in Scandinavia.

Discovering Vínland

There are many Viking sagas, or legends, that give us clues about
Viking life. There are even sagas about the Vikings in North America.
In one, a man called Bjarni Herjolfsson sailed for Greenland about
1,000 years ago, but lost his way. He found the northern coast of
Canada instead, then went back home. He told Leif
Eriksson what he had seen.

Eriksson followed his route in the same
boat a few years later. He traveled along the
North American coast, landing in a
place he called Vínland. The
name means Wineland.

Evidence of Vikings was found at L'Anse aux Meadows, the present-day province of Newfoundland. The location looks nothing like the Vínland Eriksson described. There are wild berries growing there but no grapes.

The Vikings likely traveled across a large area that included both L'Anse aux Meadows and areas farther south where grapes grew. Eriksson and his men spent the winter at L'Anse aux Meadows and built houses. In the spring they went home to Greenland.

Later on, families came to Vínland. The sagas disagree on how many people came, and whether they stayed in the same place. They agree that 60 to 160 people lived for two to three years in North America.

The Native Americans wanted to trade with the Vikings, but also attacked them. Both needed the same farmland to survive. The Native Americans may have driven the Vikings away. Nobody knows why they left, but by 1012, the Vikings had all gone home.

Viking Traders

Vikings used their ships to take trade goods along the rivers that ran into Russia. They took wax, honey, slaves, and furs to trade for luxuries such as jewelry, wine, silk, and spices. Many grew wealthy this way. Other Vikings just traded for things they needed. Vikings used things they grew or made to get what they needed from other countries.

Vikings went as far as Constantinople and Baghdad (see map on page 6) to trade their goods. They traded with merchants from Africa, Asia, and China.

Silver and gold were used as money. People hacked pieces off coins or jewelry. This "hacksilver" was weighed to pay for goods.

In Greenland and Iceland, wood was scarce. The Vikings took dried fish to England and the rest of Europe to trade for wood, which they needed for houses and boats. Farmers and craftsmen used the markets in towns such as Hedeby in Denmark.

A bronze Buddah statue was found in Sweden. It was made in India 1,500 years ago and was part of a Viking trade.

Craftspeople

Even though they made most of what they ate and wore, Viking families needed some things made for them.

Craftspeople made everyday things such as shoes, swords, bowls, cooking pots, and combs. Vikings also liked to dress nicely and have decorations. At markets they could buy glass beads, jewelry, and complicated carvings.

In later Viking times, coins started to be used as money. Each town had a mint licensed by the king to strike coins. Coins were made by hammering a mold onto a blank piece of metal.

Blacksmiths made tools and weapons. Swords were made by twisting iron and steel rods together, then hammering them flat. Both edges were then sharpened.

Craftspeople learned their trades as apprentices or from their parents. Most were men, but all women knew how to weave cloth. The finest weavings were used to decorate the edges of tunics.

Craftspeople lived in market towns where they could easily sell their goods. Mostly they traded with Vikings who lived nearby. Some traveling salesmen visited people who lived too far away to get to town.

Viking Gods

The Vikings believed in many gods. They did not always have churches or priests. Christianity did not spread until later in Viking times. Vikings believed in a kind of heaven and hell. To get to Valhalla, or heaven, a warrior had to die in battle. Viking gods lived in Asgard.

In Asgard, Odin rode a horse called Sleipnir, who had eight legs. Thor's hammer and chariot made storms as he rode through the sky. Loki caused mischief. Yggdrasil was the tree of life. The three old Norn sisters sat at its roots and spun the threads of life and death. Each thread stood for one life. A serpent called Nidhogg gnawed the roots of the tree.

Loki

24

Jewelers made crosses and Thor's hammers in the same molds. Viking traders often wore both so they could trade with Christians.

Thor

The Yggdrasil tree

The Norns

The most ancient of the gods were the twins, Frey and Freya. They were the gods of fertility. Odin was the head of the gods in Valhalla. His son Thor, the god of strength, was the most popular god.

Nidhogg

People wore Thor's hammer charms for good luck. It was also the custom for brides and grooms to make their vows on a Thor's hammer (left).

Festivals and Feasts

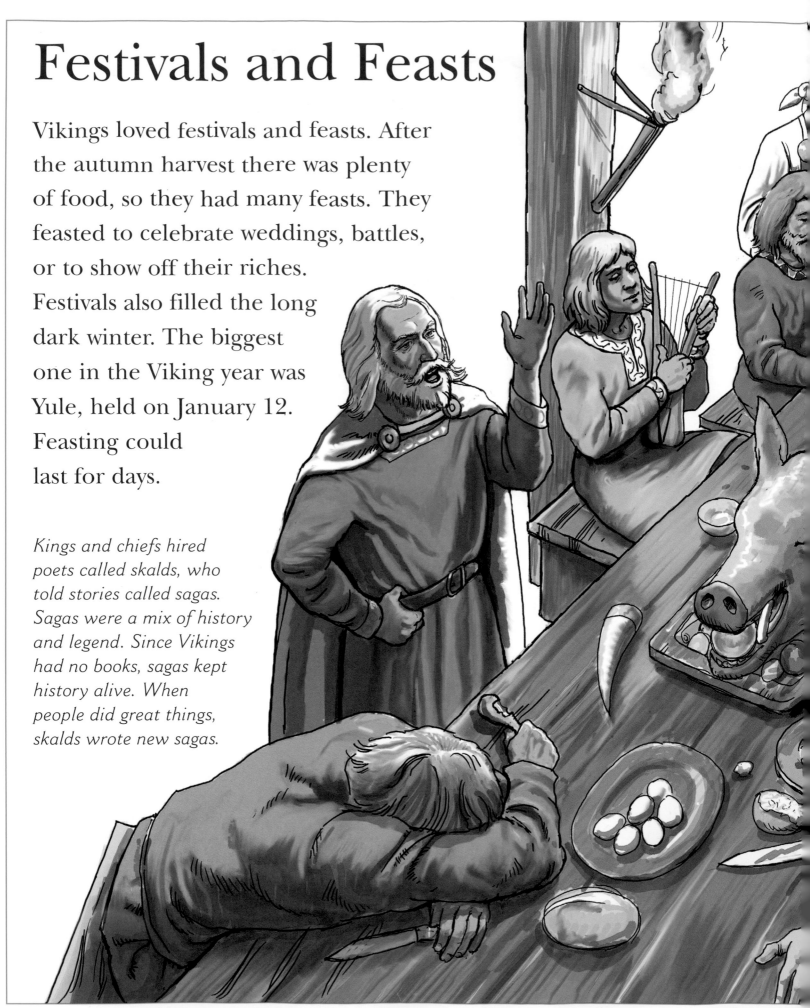

Vikings loved festivals and feasts. After the autumn harvest there was plenty of food, so they had many feasts. They feasted to celebrate weddings, battles, or to show off their riches. Festivals also filled the long dark winter. The biggest one in the Viking year was Yule, held on January 12. Feasting could last for days.

Kings and chiefs hired poets called skalds, who told stories called sagas. Sagas were a mix of history and legend. Since Vikings had no books, sagas kept history alive. When people did great things, skalds wrote new sagas.

In the winter, ice-skating and sledding were good ways to get around. They could also be fun. Viking people had ice-skating races.

People ate and drank, and listened to skalds and musicians. Contests and bets added to the fun. Some blood feuds between families began after fights at feasts. At feasts, the women did the cooking and serving.

Vikings enjoyed board games, especially to pass the time in winter. Two walrus-tusk chess pieces came from the Isle of Lewis off Scotland.

What Happened to the Vikings?

Vikings believed that the dead sailed to the next life in a ship. Rich people were buried in real ships. Poorer people were buried in graves marked by stones laid in the shape of a ship. All were laid out in their best clothes, with food and their finest things alongside them. These would help them in the afterlife.

Rich people, like the queen buried in a ship found in Oseberg, Norway, had fine things for the afterlife. Animals, a slave, cooking pots, furniture, and weapons were found in her grave.

An Arab traveler wrote about one splendid Viking funeral he saw. A chief was laid out in his boat. Then his boat was set alight. A feast celebrated his great deeds. Vikings believed that burning the dead sent their spirits straight up to heaven.

In the Scottish island of Lerwick, people still celebrate a Viking boat-burning festival called Up-Helly-Aa in January each year.

The Viking age came to an end about 900 years ago, as Europe changed and Christianity overtook old Viking beliefs. The people they had once raided had built castles to protect themselves and formed armies. Also, many Vikings had made new homes in the lands they settled.

Glossary

afterlife—the life that begins when a person dies

ammonia—the smelly chemical in urine that can kill germs

apprentice—a person who works for and learns from a skilled tradesperson for a certain amount of time

chain mail—a kind of armor made from links of metal joined to make a tunic

culture—a group of people's beliefs, customs, and way of life

runes—Viking writing, made straight up and down to be easy to carve into wood and stone

Scandinavia—the part of northern Europe that includes Norway, Denmark, and Sweden

sod—grass growing in a layer of earth, often used to make walls and roofs of houses

Thing—meeting to make laws and bring people together

trade—the buying and selling of goods such as jewelry and food

tradition—a group of people's longtime ways of doing things

Further Resources

AT THE LIBRARY

Burgan, Michael. *Leif Eriksson*. Chicago: Heinemann Library, 2002.

Schomp, Virginia. *The Vikings*. New York: Franklin Watts, 2005.

Weintraub, Aileen. *Vikings: Raiders and Explorers*. New York: Children's Press, 2005.

ON THE WEB

For more information on *The Vikings*, use FactHound

to track down Web sites related to this book.

1. Go to *www.facthound.com*

2. Type in a search word related to this book
   or this book ID: 0756516781

3. Click on the *Fetch It* button.

FactHound will find the best Web sites for you.

LOOK FOR MORE BOOKS IN THIS SERIES

ANCIENT MAYA
ISBN 0-7565-1677-3

ANCIENT ROMANS
ISBN 0-7565-1644-7

ANCIENT GREEKS
ISBN 0-7565-1646-3

Index